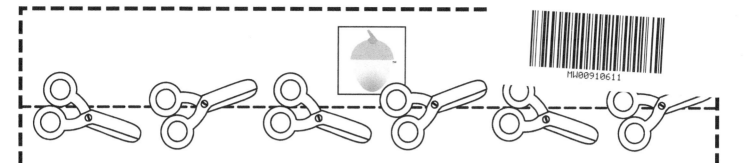

SNIP SNIP
Early Cutting Skills

by Marilynn G. Barr

Reproduce and cut out this award for children as they master their scissor skills.

Congratulations,

_____
Name

is a

SNIP SNIP EXPERT!

This certificate is awarded for mastering scissor skills.

_____
Teacher   Date

LAB20131
SNIP SNIP
by Marilynn G. Barr

Published by: Little Acorn Books™
Originally published by: Monday Morning Books, Inc.

Entire contents copyright © 2013 Little Acorn Books™

Little Acorn Books
PO Box 8787
Greensboro,NC 27419-0787

Promoting Early Skills for a Lifetime™

Little Acorn Books™
is an imprint of Little Acorn Associates, Inc.

http://www.littleacornbooks.com

ISBN 978-1-937257-17-0

Printed in the United States of America

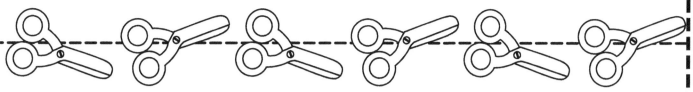

Snip Snip

Contents

Introduction.. 4

    Snip Snip Mobiles

    Snip Snip Collages

    Snip Snip Flags

    Snip Snip Puzzles

    Snip Snip Props and Puppets

    Snip Snip Picture Books

Snip Snip Activities

    I Can Cut Out Ladybug Shapes 7

    I Can Make a Ladybug.......................... 8

    I Can Cut Out Castle Shapes 9

    I Can Build a Castle 10

    I Can Cut Out Fruit Shapes 11

    I Can Fill a Fruit Bowl.........................12

    I Can Cut Out Shells 13

    I Can Fill a Sand Pail 14

    I Can Cut Out Buildings.......................15

    I Can Build a City 16

    I Can Cut Out Flower Shapes 17

    I Can Make a Flower 18

    I Can Cut Out Octopus Shapes 19

    I Can Make an Octopus 20

    I Can Cut Out Stars............................21

    I Can Make a Flag 22

    I Can Cut Out Butterfly Shapes 23

    I Can Make a Butterfly.......................24

    I Can Cut Out Fish Shapes...................25

    I Can Make a Fish 26

    I Can Put a Fish in the Bowl 27

    I Can Cut Out Bird Shapes...................28

    I Can Make Birds 29

    I Can Put a Bird in the Nest 30

    I Can Cut Out Dog Shapes...................31

    I Can Make a Dog...............................32

I Can Put a Dog in the Dog House........33

I Can Cut Out Cat Shapes 34

I Can Make a Cat................................35

I Can Cut Out Caterpillar Shapes........36

I Can Make a Caterpillar.....................37

I Can Cut Out Eggs............................38

I Can Fill the Basket With Eggs 39

I Can Cut Out Rainbow Shapes............40

I Can Make a Rainbow 41

I Can Cut Out Sailboat Shapes 42

I Can Build a Sailboat 43

I Can Cut Out Clothes 44

I Can Pack a Suitcase 45

I Can Cut Out Circus Animals 46

I Can Cut Out Circus Train Engine

    Shapes 47

I Can Build a Circus Train Engine.........48

I Can Cut Out Box Car Shapes............49

I Can Build a Box Car 50

I Can Cut Out Hot Air Balloon

    Shapes 51

I Can Make a Hot Air Balloon 52

I Can Cut Out Elephant Shapes 53

I Can Make an Elephant 54

I Can Cut Out Carousel Animals...........55

I Can Cut Out Carousel Shapes............56

I Can Build a Carousel 57

I Can Cut Out Clown Shapes 58

I Can Make a Clown 59

I Can Cut Out Robot Shapes................60

I Can Build a Robot.............................61

I Can Cut Out Airplane Shapes............62

I Can Build an Airplane........................63

Cutting Practice Sheets.........................64

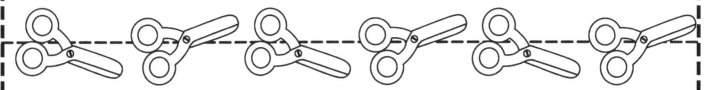

Snip Snip Introduction

Snip Snip activities provide plenty of creative hands-on readiness skills practice. Children practice cutting, matching, and pasting geometric and free- form shapes. Patterns include shape cutouts to build castles, cities, and sailboats. Children will enjoy packing suitcases, creating pets, and loading circus trains. Projects are designed for beginning as well as advanced learners. Easy-to-follow directions offer advanced learners reading practice. Nonreaders can complete projects with oral direction. Activity sheets range from easy to challenging. Every project reinforces hand-eye coordination and fine motor skills development. Project themes also offer early language skills development. Children can tell stories about their pets or packing for a vacation. Invite youngsters to participate in discussions about bugs, pets, the circus, and more.

Each activity includes one page of shapes to color and cut out and a second outline page to glue on matching shapes. Options are listed at the bottom of each activity page. Children can make shape books and storage pockets from outline patterns. Optional materials such as pom poms, sequins, and cereal Os can transform projects into works of art.

Cutting Practice Sheets (p. 64) are also included.

Snip Snip Activities

Provide children with crayons, scissors, and glue to assemble the activities found in Snip Snip. Two-page activities include patterns to cut out and glue on match boards. Cut away the option at the bottom of the assembled outline page. Invite each child, in turn, to tell a story about his or her completed project. Encourage children to include descriptive words in their stories. For example: My ladybug is <u>red</u>. It has <u>six</u> <u>black</u> spots. My ladybug has <u>six</u> legs. I glued <u>two</u> pipe cleaner antenna on my ladybug.

Provide children with materials to create colorful displays, puppets, and props.

Note: For young children, cut out the shapes and let the children glue them on the match board on the correct spaces.

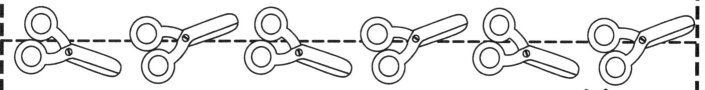

Snip Snip Mobiles

Provide each child with a paper towel tube. Have children use crayons or markers to decorate their tubes. Children can also decorate tubes with glue, glitter, and gift wrap scraps. Provide each child with a matching set of Snip Snip activity sheets. For example, reproduce the shells and sand pail (pp. 13-14). Have children assemble, then cut out their sand pails filled with shells. Help each child punch a hole at the top of his or her sand pail cutout. Cut, lace, and tie a length of yarn through the hole. Then tie the loose end around the center of the decorated paper towel tube and secure with tape. Cut another length of yarn long enough to thread and tie loosely through the tube. Hang the sand pail mobile from a door frame or ceiling.

Snip Snip Collages

Prepare a table with crayons, markers, scissors, glue, and a variety of craft supplies (beads, sand, buttons, cloth scraps, newspaper). Each child will need a sheet of colored construction paper or colored poster board. Provide children with a combination of shapes pages. Example: shells, fish, and sailboat shapes (pp. 13, 25, 42). Help children trace and cut out shapes

from cloth scraps. Children can glue buttons, sand, or beads on the shape cutouts. Then help each child assemble and glue the shape cutouts to create a beach collage.

Snip Snip Flags

Each child will need a construction paper flag outline (p. 22) to cut out. Reproduce a variety of shapes pages for children to choose from. Have children color and cut out their shapes. Help each child assemble and glue his or her shapes on the flag. Then have the child dictate a slogan or message to write on the flag. Staple or glue a large craft stick to the back of each child's flag. Option: Staple a length of yarn to the short straight edge of the flag to form a banner. Display flags or banners on a bulletin board.

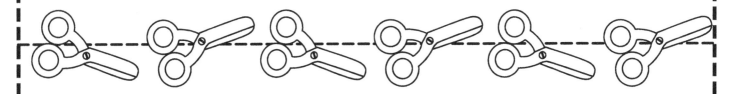

Snip Snip Puzzles

Reproduce, color, and cut out each set of Snip Snip Activity pages from oak tag. Glue each outline and an envelope for shapes storage to the inside of a folder. Write the activity title, then decorate the front of the folder. Younger children can practice placing the shapes on the outline. Older and advanced learners can practice assembling the shapes on the back of the closed folder.

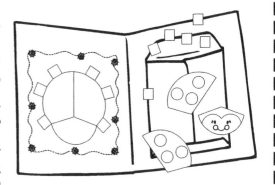

Snip Snip Props and Puppets

Prepare a workstation with small bags, large craft sticks, crayons, scissors, glue, and tape. Reproduce activity pages (castle, city, flower, suitcase, or carousel) for children to make props. Help children glue or staple craft sticks to the backs of cutouts. Castles can be used during fairy tale readings. Cities, sailboats, and carousels can be used to tell about a field trip or vacation.

Reproduce activity pages (ladybug, octopus, butterfly) for children to make puppets. Help children glue or staple craft sticks to the backs of cutouts to form stick puppets. Cutouts can also be glued on small paper bags to form hand puppets.

Snip Snip Picture Books

Provide each child with a set of Snip Snip activity pages to color, cut out, and assemble. Cut away the option at the bottom of the assembled outline page. When children have accumulated several finished projects, help them form Snip Snip Picture Books. Have children decorate construction paper covers for their books. Punch two holes along the left margin of each page and book cover. Cut, lace, and tie a length of yarn through the holes to form each child's book.

My Snip Snip Book

I Can Cut Out Ladybug Shapes

Trace the shapes. Cut out the shapes.

Options:
- Glue black pom poms on the dots.
- Decorate, cut out, and glue a craft stick to the back of a ladybug outline to form a stick puppet.

I Can Make a Ladybug

Glue ladybug shapes on this page.

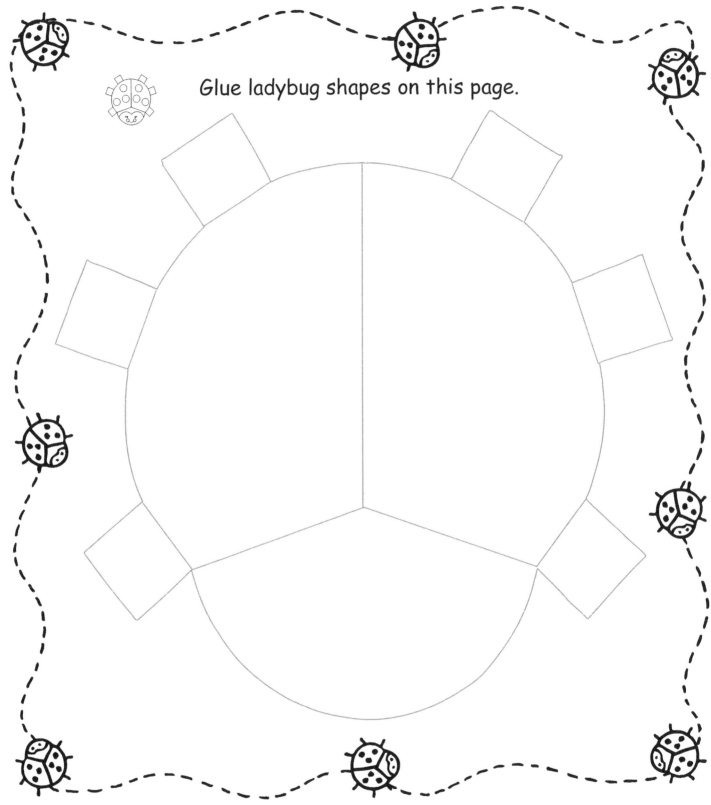

 Options:
- Glue on the six legs first, then the wings in a flying position as shown on the left.
- Reproduce, cut out, and staple ten ladybug outlines together to form a book.

I Can Cut Out Castle Shapes

Trace the shapes. Cut out the shapes.

Options:
- Paint on glue, then sprinkle sand on the castle shapes.
- Reproduce and cut out the castle shapes from fine sand paper, felt, or craft foam.

I Can Build a Castle

Glue castle shapes on this page.

Options:
- Decorate, cut out, and glue castle outlines to cereal boxes.
- Cut and glue corrugated board bricks on castle outlines.
- Reproduce, cut out, and staple ten castle outlines together to form a book.

I Can Cut Out Fruit Shapes

Trace the shapes. Cut out the shapes.

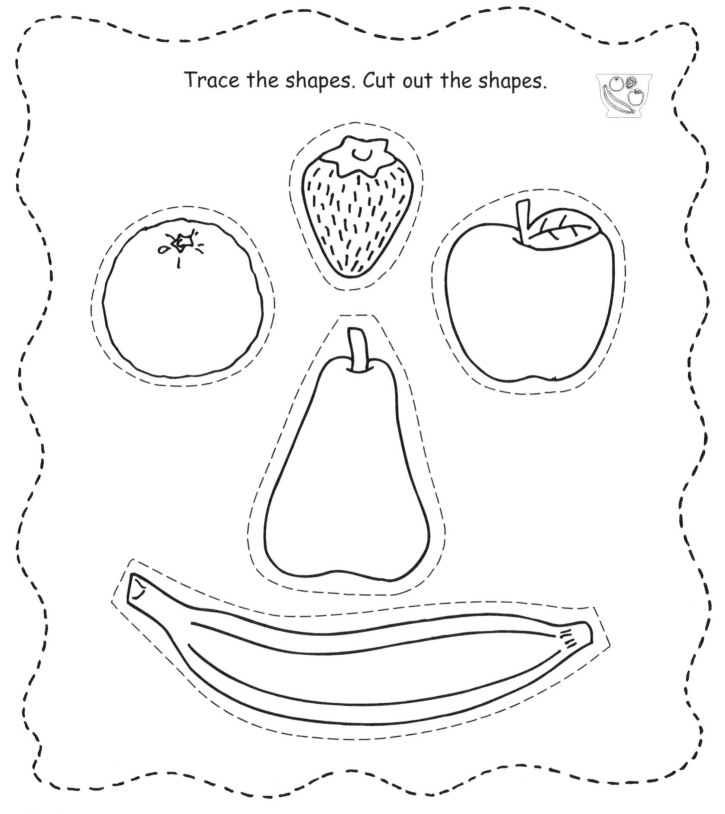

Options:
• Glue small colored pom poms on each fruit.
• Draw faces, then glue craft sticks to the backs of fruit cutouts to form stick puppets.

I Can Fill a Fruit Bowl

Glue fruit shapes in the bowl.

Option:
- Decorate, cut out, and tape or staple two bowl outlines together along the bottom and sides to form a storage pocket.

I Can Cut Out Shells

Trace the shapes. Cut out the shapes.

Options:
- Paint on glue, then sprinkle glitter or sand on shells.
- Reproduce and program the backs of two sets of shells with letters or numbers to use as flash or game cards.

I Can Fill a Sand Pail

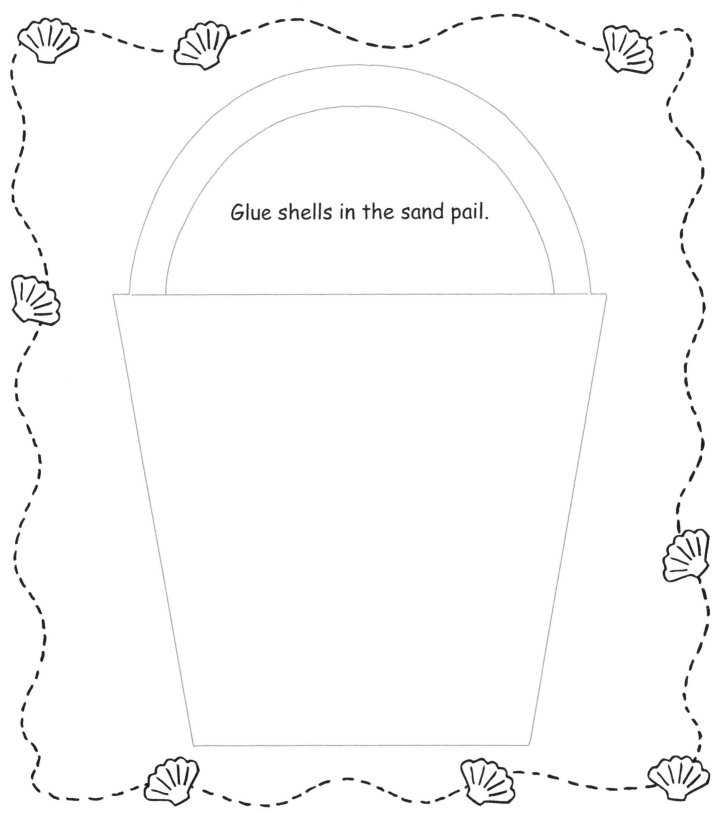

Glue shells in the sand pail.

Options:
- Reproduce, cut out, and staple ten sand pail outlines together to form a book.
- Decorate, cut out, and tape or staple two sand pail outlines along the bottom and sides to form a storage pocket.

I Can Cut Out Buildings

Trace the shapes.
Cut out the shapes.

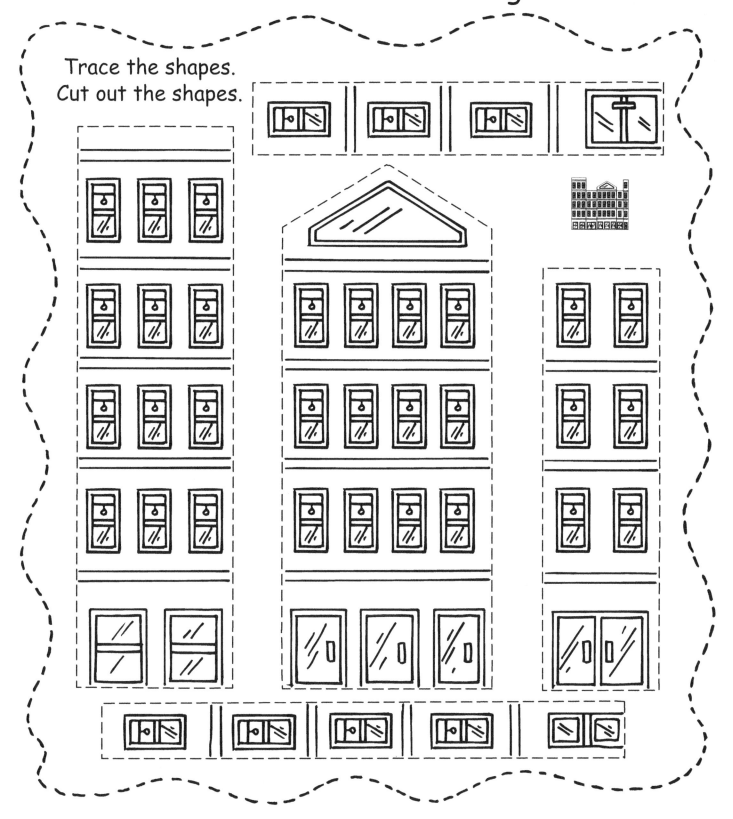

Options:
- Glue building shapes to boxes and paper towel tubes to make a 3-D city.
- Reproduce and cut out the buildings from felt, cloth scraps, gift wrap, or craft foam.

I Can Build a City

Glue buildings on this page.

Options:
- Reproduce, cut out, and staple ten city outlines together to form a book.
- Use chalk to draw doors and windows on black construction paper city outlines.

I Can Cut Out Flower Shapes

Trace the shapes. Cut out the shapes.

Options:
• Glue rice or elbow macaroni on flower shapes.
• Reproduce and cut out the flower shapes from felt, cloth scraps, gift wrap, or craft foam.

I Can Make a Flower

Glue flower shapes on this page.

Options:
- Cut and glue a brown grocery bag flower pot along the bottom of a sheet of construction paper. Decorate, then glue a flower outline at the top of the flower pot.
- Decorate, cut out, and glue a paint stirrer to the back of a flower outline.

I Can Cut Out Octopus Shapes

Trace the shapes.
Cut out the shapes.

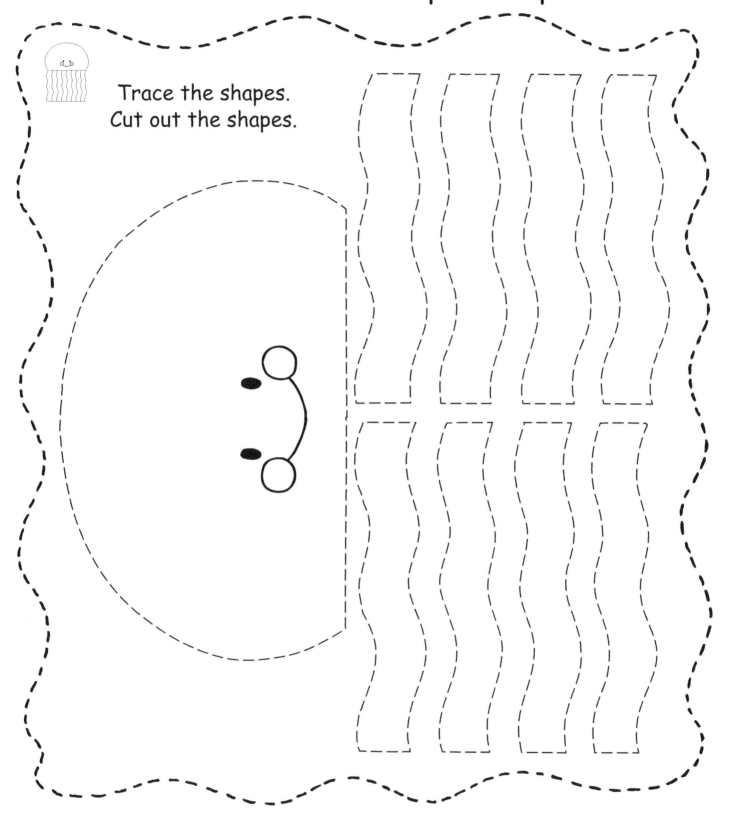

Options:
- Cut out, then glue cereal Os on the octopus shapes.
- Reproduce and cut out the octopus shapes from felt, cloth scraps, gift wrap, or craft foam.

I Can Make an Octopus

Glue octopus shapes on this page.

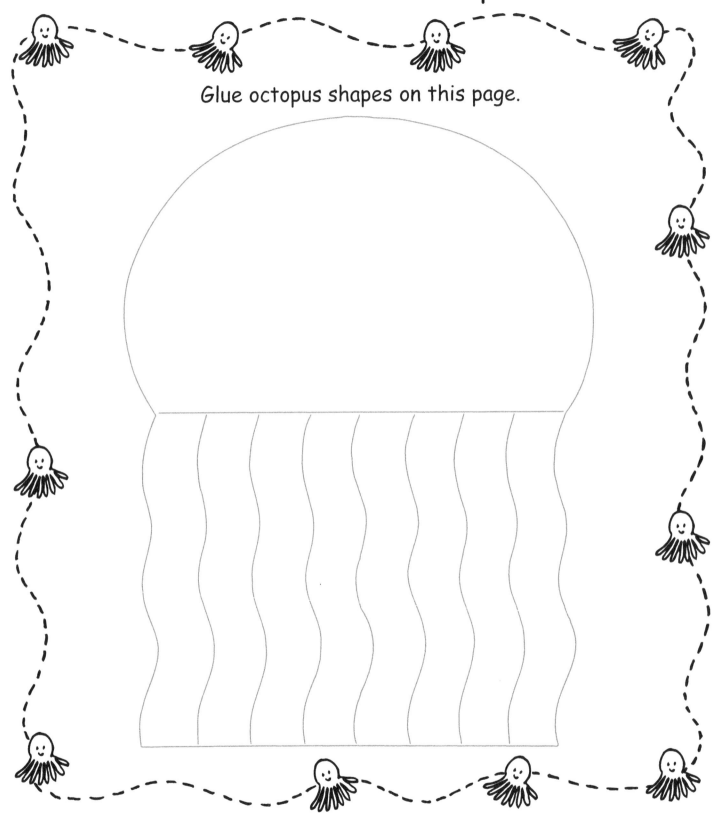

Options:
- Use chalk to decorate a black construction paper octopus outline.
- Cut out, then glue or staple a craft stick to the back of an octopus outline to form a stick puppet.

I Can Cut Out Stars

Trace the stars. Cut out the stars.

Options:
• Trace and cut out foil stars to glue on a flag outline.
• Reproduce and cut out the stars from felt, cloth scraps, gift wrap, or craft foam.

I Can Make a Flag

Glue stars on the flag.

Options:
- Reproduce, cut out, and staple ten flag outlines together to form a book.
- Decorate, cut out, and glue or staple a paint stirrer along the back straight edge of a flag.

I Can Cut Out Butterfly Shapes

Trace the shapes.
Cut out the shapes.

Options:
- Trace and cut out the butterfly shapes from colored cellophane.
- Reproduce and cut out the butterfly shapes from felt, cloth scraps, gift wrap, or craft foam.

I Can Make a Butterfly

Glue butterfly shapes on this page.

Options:
- Reproduce, cut out, and staple ten butterfly outlines together to form a book.
- Decorate, cut out, and glue or staple a craft stick to the back of a butterfly outline to form a stick puppet. Then attach two pipe cleaner antennae.

I Can Cut Out Fish Shapes

Trace the shapes. Cut out the shapes.

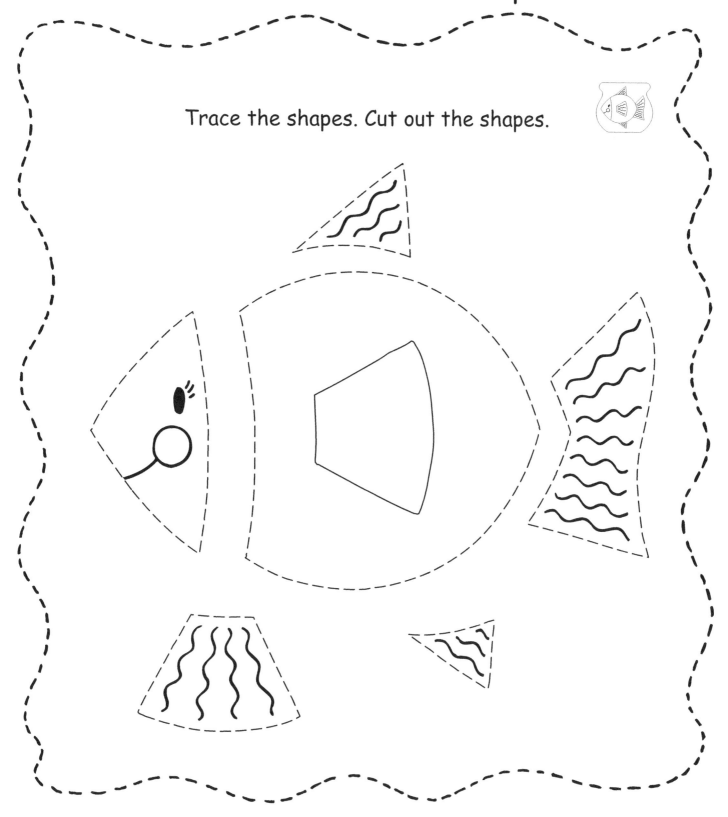

Options:
- Glue sequins on the fish shapes.
- Reproduce and cut out fish shapes from felt, cloth scraps, gift wrap, or craft foam.

I Can Make a Fish

Glue fish shapes on this page.

Options:
- Decorate, cut out, and glue or staple a craft stick to the back of a fish outline to form a stick puppet.
- Reproduce, decorate, and cut out three fish outlines to make a mobile.

I Can Put a Fish in the Bowl

Trace the bowl. Glue a fish in the bowl.

Options:
- Reproduce, cut out, and staple ten fish bowl outlines together to form a book.
- Draw one to ten fish on each page to make a counting book.

I Can Cut Out Bird Shapes

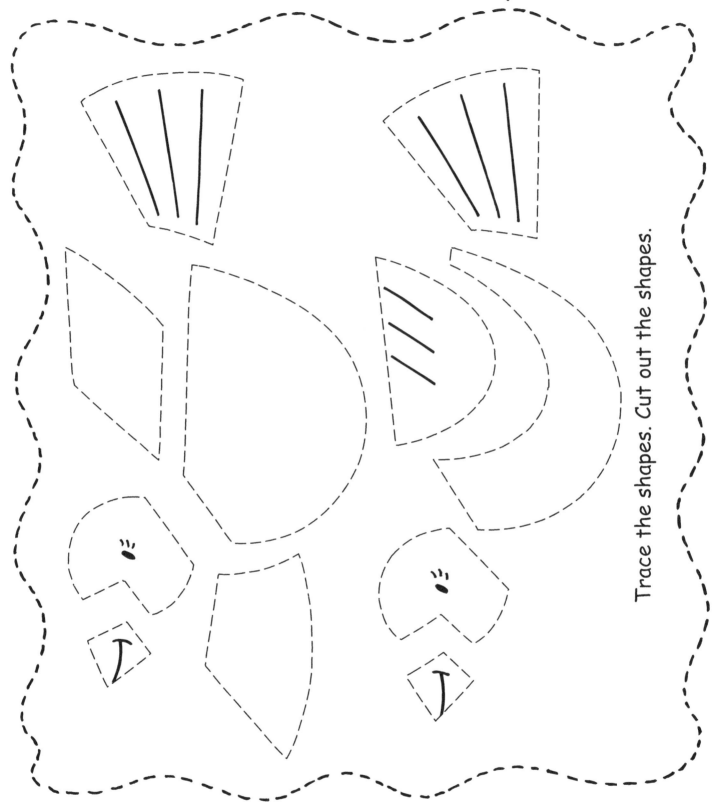

Trace the shapes. Cut out the shapes.

Options:
• Cut and glue colorful yarn on the bird shapes. Glue craft feathers on the bird shapes.
• Reproduce and cut out bird shapes from felt, cloth scraps, gift wrap, or craft foam.

I Can Make Birds

Glue bird shapes on this page.

Options:
- Decorate, cut out, and glue or staple a craft stick to the back of each bird outline to form a stick puppet.
- Reproduce, decorate, and cut out three flying bird outlines to make a mobile.

I Can Put a Bird in the Nest

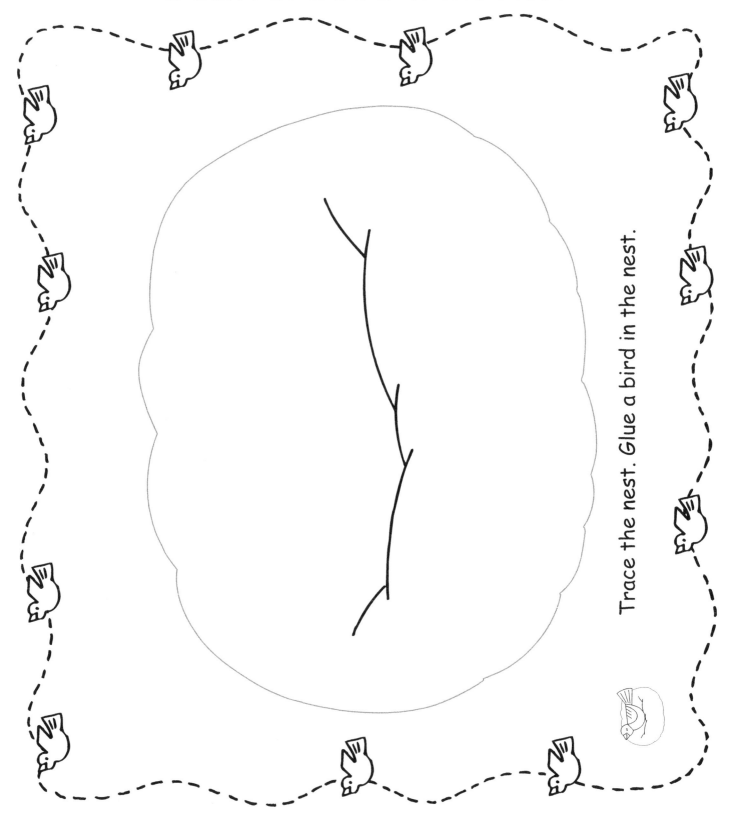

Trace the nest. Glue a bird in the nest.

Options:
- Glue twigs, yarn scraps, or straw on a nest outline.
- Reproduce, cut out, and staple ten nest outlines together to form a book.

I Can Cut Out Dog Shapes

Trace the shapes. Cut out the shapes.

Options:
- Glue pom poms or yarn on the dog shapes.
- Reproduce and cut out dog shapes from felt, fake fur, cloth scraps, gift wrap, or craft foam.

I Can Make a Dog

Glue dog shapes on this page.

Options:
- Reproduce, cut out, and staple ten dog outlines together to form a book.
- Decorate, cut out, and glue or staple a craft stick to the back of a dog outline to form a stick puppet.

I Can Put a Dog in the Dog House

Glue a dog on this page.

Options:
- Reproduce, cut out, and staple ten brown grocery bag dog house outlines to form a book.
- Decorate, cut out, and staple two dog house outlines together along the bottom and sides to form a storage pocket.

I Can Cut Out Cat Shapes

Trace the shapes. Cut out the shapes.

Options:
- Cut and glue yarn or pipe cleaner whiskers on the cat's face.
- Reproduce and cut out cat shapes from felt, cloth scraps, fake fur, gift wrap, or craft foam.

I Can Make a Cat

Glue cat shapes on this page.

Options:
- Fingerpaint a brown grocery bag cat outline.
- Decorate, cut out, and glue or staple a craft stick to the back of a cat outline to form a stick puppet.

I Can Cut Out Caterpillar Shapes

Trace the shapes. Cut out the shapes.

Options:
- Glue large pom poms on the caterpillar shapes.
- Decorate the shapes with glitter.

I Can Make a Caterpillar

Glue caterpillar shapes on this page.

Options:
- Cut and glue green yarn for grass to the background.
- Glue different-colored glitter on each section of the caterpillar.

I Can Cut Out Eggs

Trace the shapes. Cut out the shapes.

Options:
- Trace and cut out cellophane eggs. Use permanent markers to color cellophane eggs.
- Glue sequins, buttons, rice, pasta, or glitter on the eggs.
- Reproduce and cut out eggs from felt, cloth scraps, gift wrap, or craft foam.

I Can Fill the Basket With Eggs

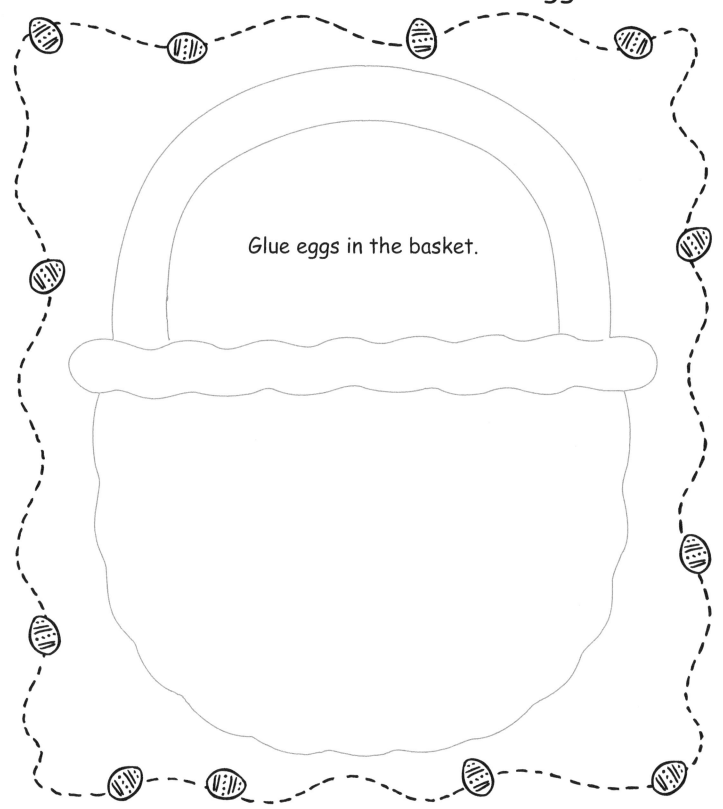

Glue eggs in the basket.

Options:
- Cut and glue ribbon on a basket outline.
- Reproduce, cut out, and staple ten basket outlines together to form a book.
- Decorate, cut out, and tape two basket outlines together to form a storage pocket.

I Can Cut Out Rainbow Shapes

Trace the shapes. Cut out the shapes.

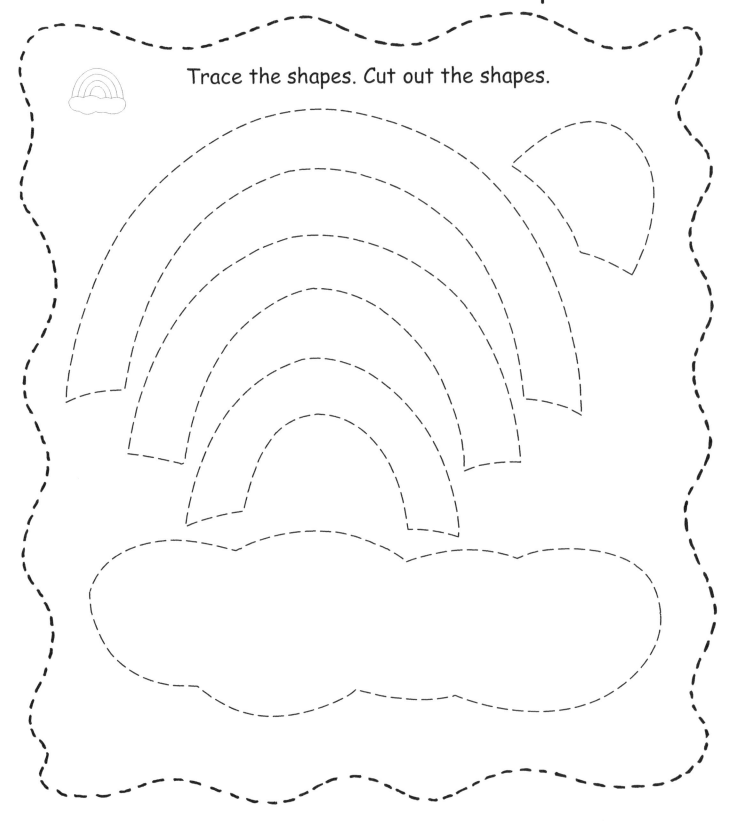

Options:
- Reproduce and cut out rainbow shapes from felt, cloth scraps, gift wrap, or craft foam.
- Paint on glue, then sprinkle glitter on the rainbow shapes.

I Can Make a Rainbow

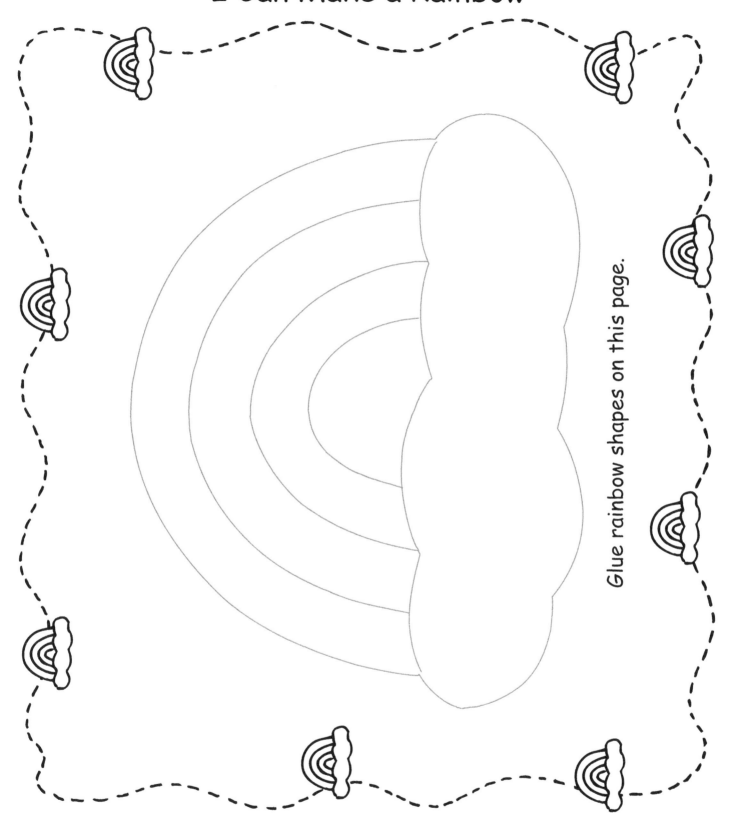

Glue rainbow shapes on this page.

Options:
- Reproduce, cut out, and staple ten rainbow outlines together to form a book.
- Decorate, cut out, and glue or staple a craft stick to the back of an oak tag rainbow outline.

I Can Cut Out Sailboat Shapes

Trace the shapes. Cut out the shapes.

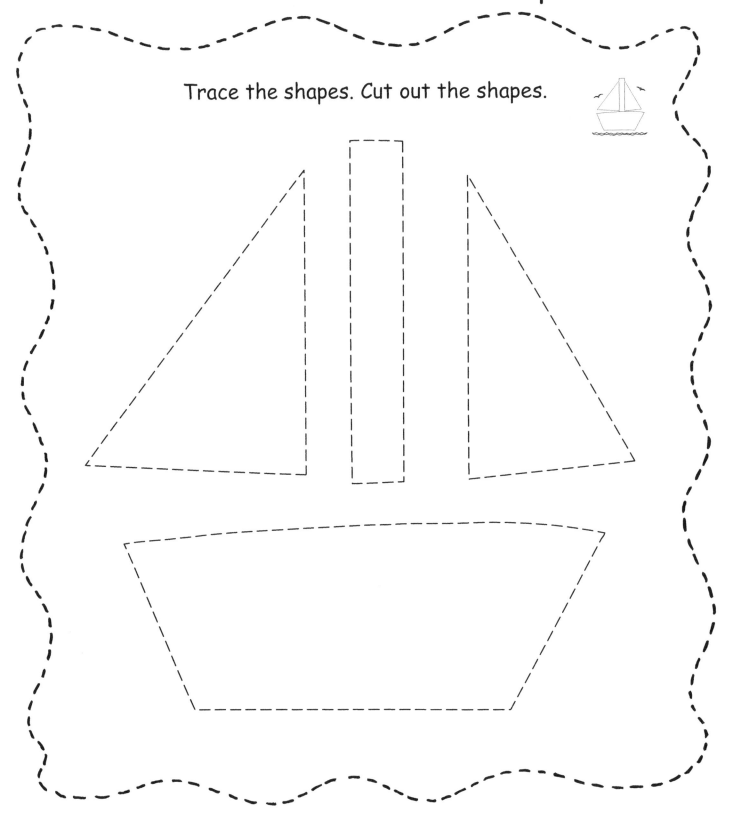

Options:
- Glue buttons, pom poms, yarn, sequins, rice, or ribbon on sailboat shapes.
- Reproduce and cut out sailboat shapes from felt, cloth scraps, gift wrap, or craft foam.

I Can Build a Sailboat

Glue sailboat shapes on this page.

Options:
- Cut and glue blue and green tissue paper waves on a sheet of oak tag or construction paper. Then decorate, cut out, and glue a sailboat on the waves.
- Decorate, cut out and glue or staple a craft stick to the back of a sailboat outline.

I Can Cut Out Clothes

Trace the shapes. Cut out the shapes.

Options:
- Reproduce and cut out clothing shapes from felt, cloth scraps, gift wrap, or craft foam.
- Decorate the clothing shapes with buttons, pom poms, glitter, sequins, craft feathers, or yarn.

I Can Pack a Suitcase

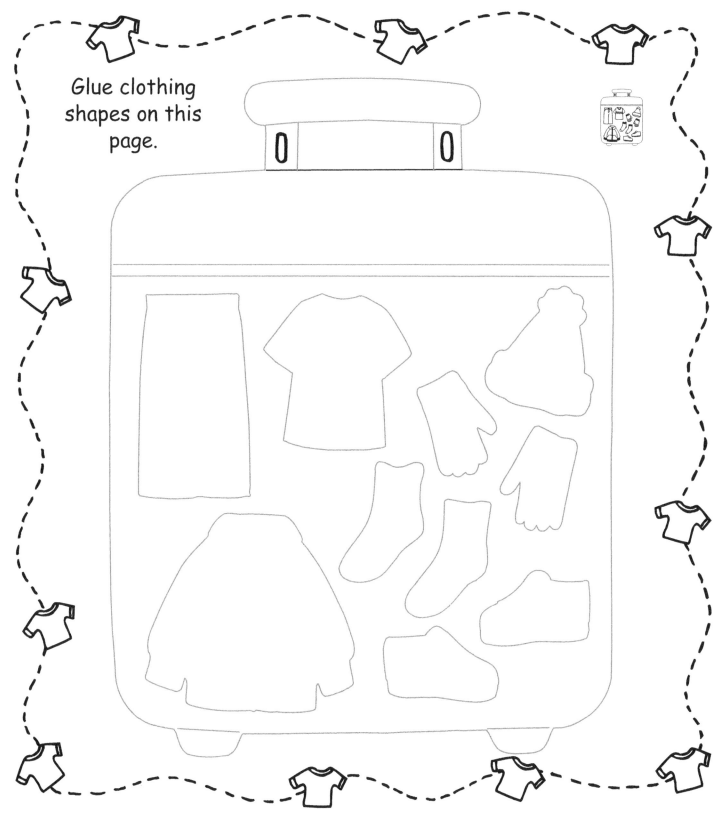

Glue clothing shapes on this page.

Options:
- Reproduce, cut out, and staple ten suitcase outlines together to form a book.
- Decorate, cut out, and tape or staple two suitcase outlines together to form a storage pocket.

I Can Cut Out Circus Animals

Trace the shapes. Cut out the shapes.

Options:
- Reproduce and cut out circus animals from felt, cloth scraps, fake fur, or craft foam.
- Glue a craft stick to the back of each circus animal to form stick puppets.

I Can Cut Out Circus Train Engine Shapes

Trace the shapes. Cut out the shapes.

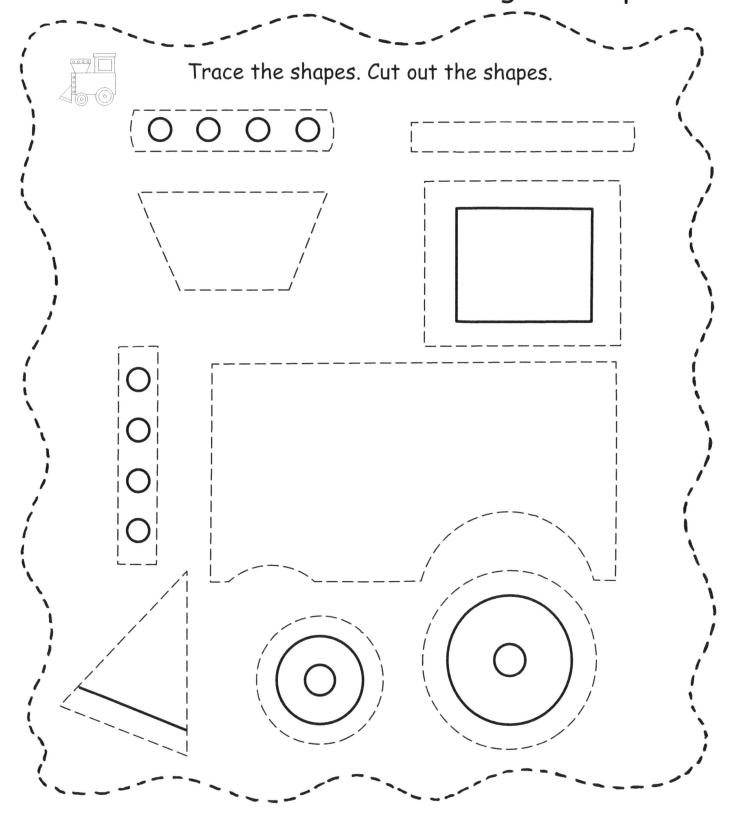

Options:
- Reproduce and cut out engine shapes from felt, gift wrap, or craft foam.
- Cut and glue foil details on the engine outline.

I Can Build a Circus Train Engine

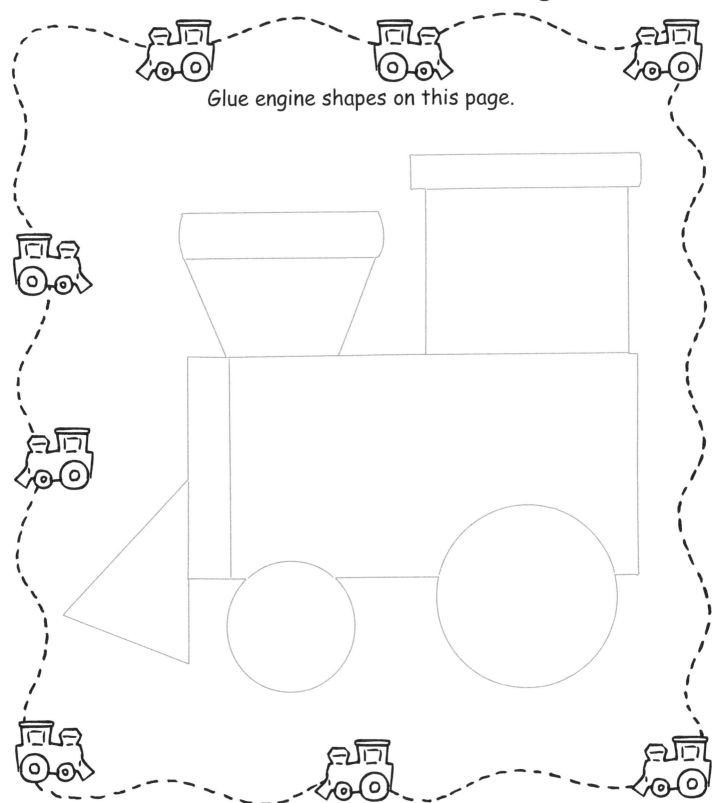

Glue engine shapes on this page.

Options:
- Reproduce, cut out, and staple ten engine outlines together to form a book.
- Decorate, cut out, and glue or staple a craft stick to the back of an oak tag engine outline.

I Can Cut Out Box Car Shapes

Trace the shapes. Cut out the shapes.

Options:
• Reproduce and cut out box car shapes from felt, cloth scraps, gift wrap, or craft foam.
• Cut and glue foil details on the box car shapes.

I Can Build a Box Car

Glue box car shapes on this page.

Options:
- Reproduce, cut out, and staple ten box car outlines together to form a book.
- Use completed engine and boxcars to make a garland.

I Can Cut Out Hot Air Balloon Shapes

Trace the shapes.
Cut out the shapes.

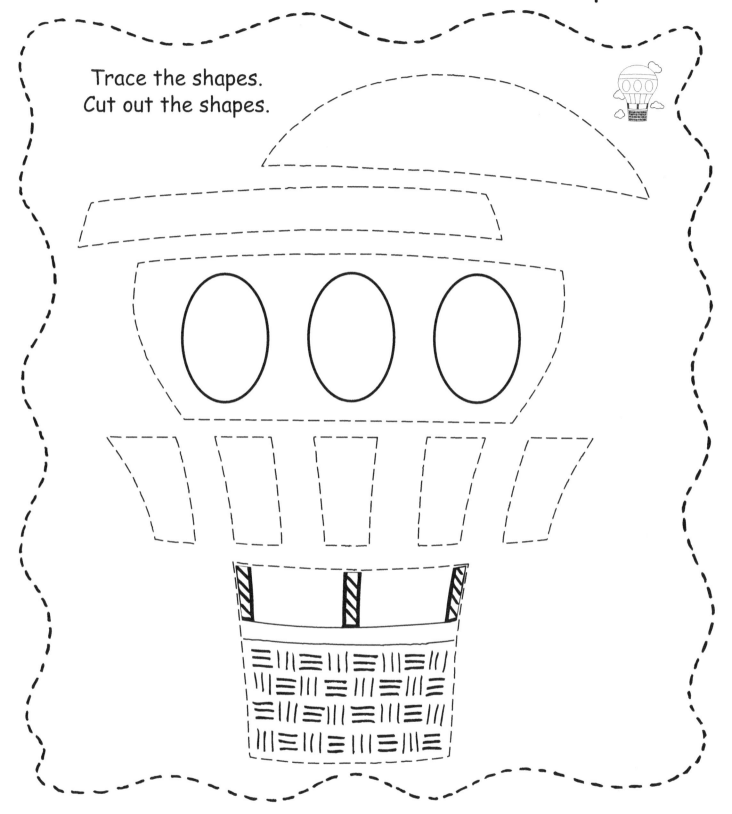

Options:
- Crumple, then glue small craft tissue squares on the hot air balloon shape cutouts.
- Reproduce and cut out hot air balloon shapes from felt, cloth scraps, gift wrap, or craft foam.

I Can Make a Hot Air Balloon

Glue hot air balloon shapes on this page.

Options:
- Reproduce, cut out, and staple ten hot air balloon outlines together to form a book.
- Decorate, cut out, punch a hole, then lace and tie a length of yarn to the top of a hot air balloon outline for hanging.

I Can Cut Out Elephant Shapes

Trace the shapes. Cut out the shapes.

Options:
- Sponge paint the elephant shapes. Then add permanent marker details.
- Reproduce and cut out elephant shapes from felt, cloth scraps, gift wrap, or craft foam.

I Can Make an Elephant

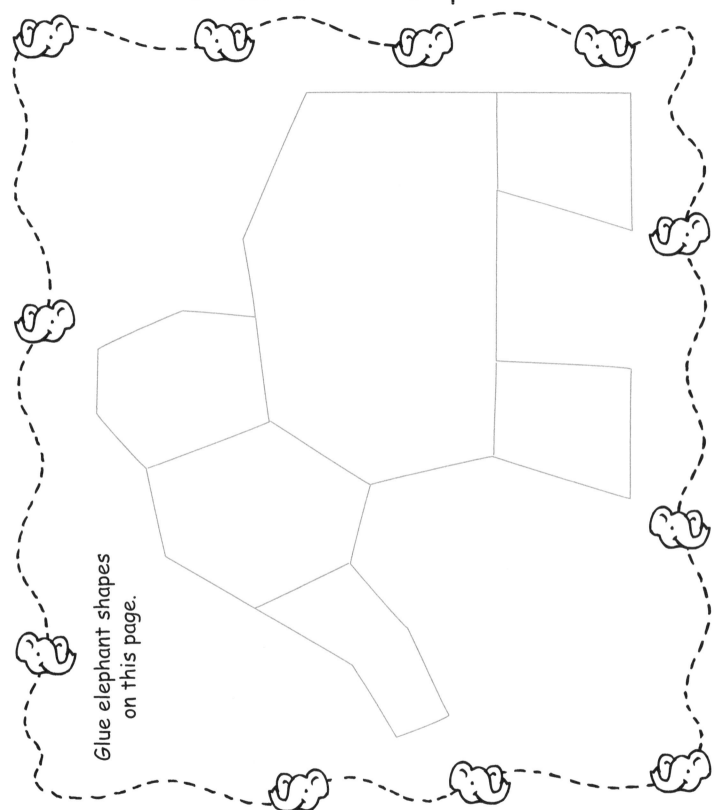

Glue elephant shapes on this page.

Options:
- Draw and color a blanket on an elephant outline.
- Decorate, cut out, and glue or staple a craft stick to the back of an elephant outline to form a stick puppet.

I Can Cut Out Carousel Animals

Trace the shapes. Cut out the shapes.

Options:
• Glue glitter on carousel shapes.
• Use carousel shapes to decorate book covers, note books, or binders.

I Can Cut Out Carousel Shapes

Trace the shapes.
Cut out the shapes.

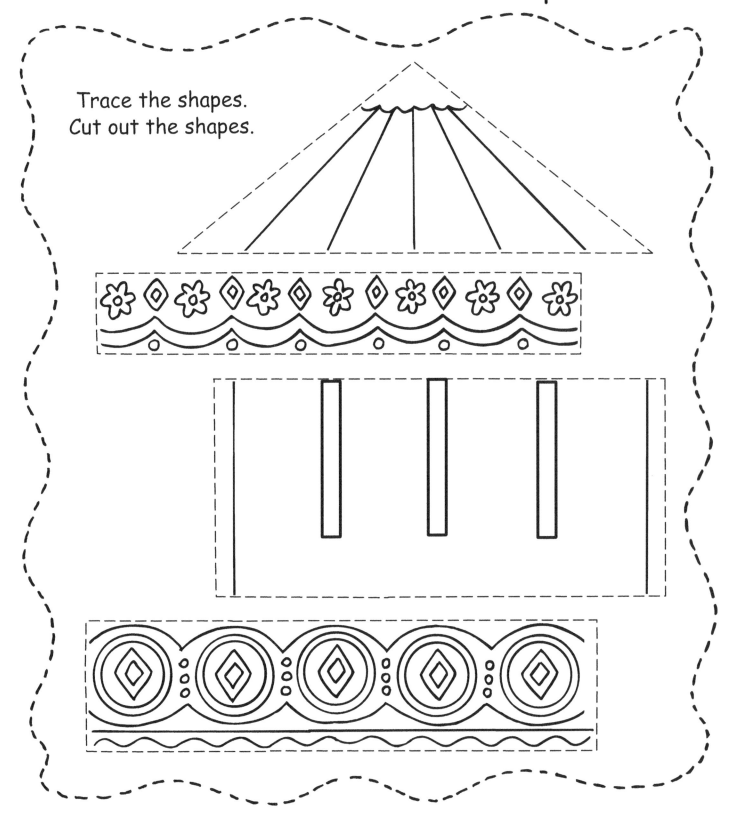

Options:
• Decorate the carousel shapes with pom poms, buttons, cereal Os, and glitter.
• Reproduce and cut out carousel shapes from felt, cloth scraps, gift wrap, or craft foam.

I Can Build a Carousel

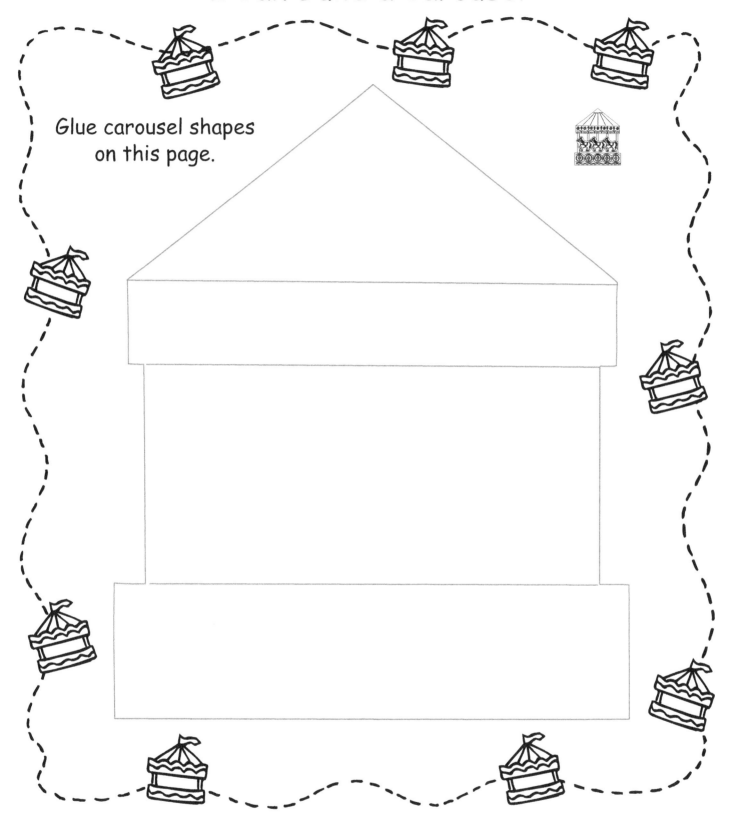

Glue carousel shapes on this page.

Options:
- Use glitter pens or glue and yarn to add details to a carousel outline.
- Use completed carousels to make bulletin board borders.

I Can Cut Out Clown Shapes

Trace the shapes. Cut out the shapes.

Options:
- Glue pom poms or buttons on the clown shapes.
- Reproduce and cut out clown shapes from felt, cloth scraps, gift wrap, or craft foam.

I Can Make a Clown

Glue clown shapes on this page.

Options:
- Use glitter pens to draw details on a clown outline.
- Decorate, cut out, and glue or staple a craft stick to the back of a clown outline to form a stick puppet.

I Can Cut Out Robot Shapes

Trace the shapes. Cut out the shapes.

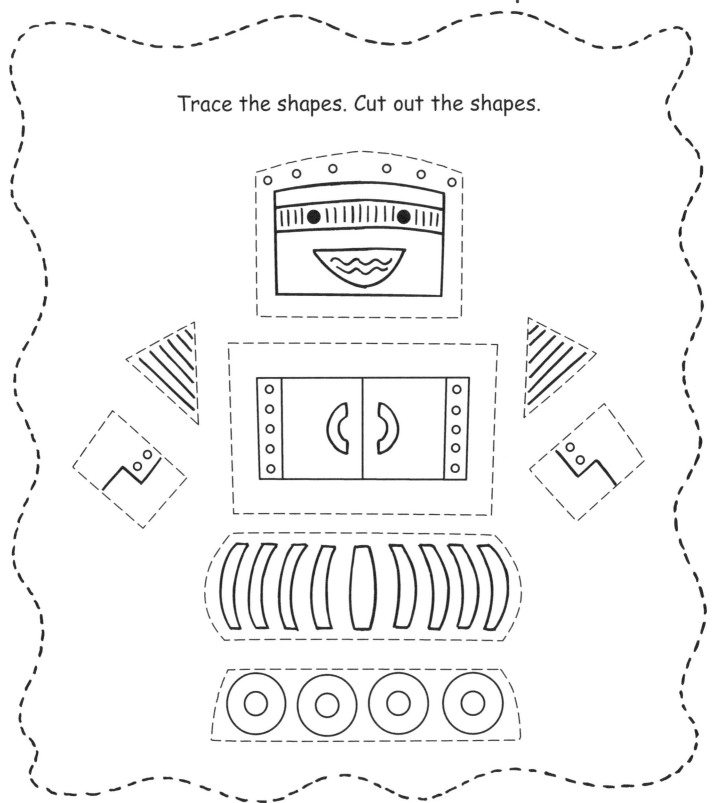

Options:
- Cut and glue foil details to the robot shapes.
- Glue buttons or beads on the robot shapes.
- Reproduce and cut out robot shapes from felt, cloth scraps, gift wrap, or craft foam.

I Can Build a Robot

Glue robot shapes on this page.

Options:
- Use glitter pens to draw details on robot outline.
- Decorate, cut out, and glue or staple a craft stick to the back of a robot outline to form a stick puppet.

I Can Cut Out Airplane Shapes

Trace the shapes. Cut out the shapes

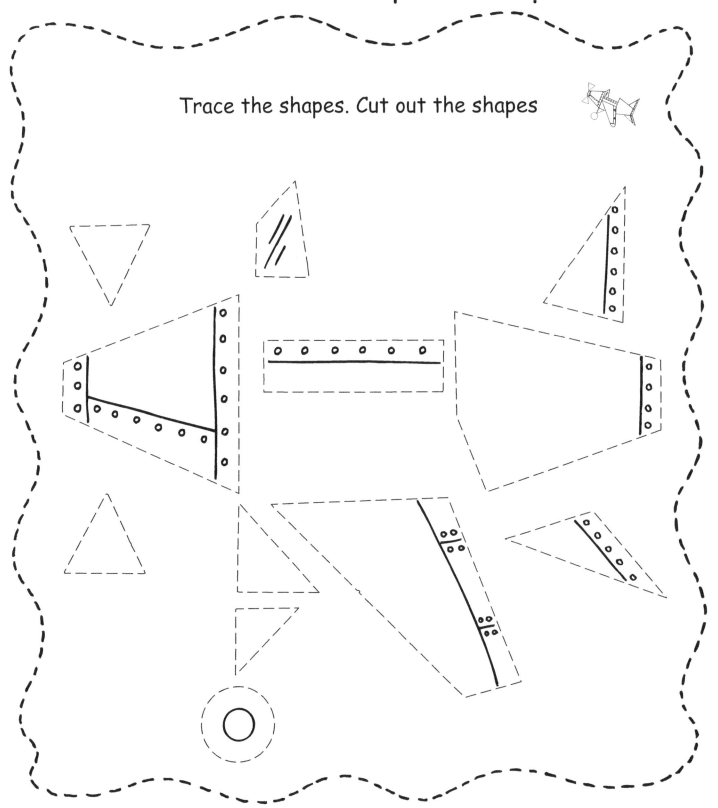

Options:
- Trace and cut out airplane shapes from clean vegetable foam trays. Use permanent markers to color the plastic foam airplane shapes.
- Reproduce and cut out airplane shapes from felt, poster board, or craft foam.

I Can Build an Airplane

Glue airplane shapes on this page.

Options:
- Make a color-by-number activity. Program each airplane shape with a numeral. Assign a different color to each numeral used in the picture, then create a legend.
- Decorate, cut out, and glue a craft stick to the back of the airplane outline.

Cutting Practice Sheets

_____ Name

Stop cutting here.

Cut along the dotted line.

Start cutting here.

_____ Name

Stop cutting here.

Cut along the dotted line.

Start cutting here.

_____ Name

Stop cutting here.

Cut along the dotted line.

Start cutting here.

_____ Name

Stop cutting here.

Cut along the dotted line.

Start cutting here.

Reproduce and cut apart a set of cutting practice sheets for each child to practice cutting on the dotted lines.

Option: Provide crayons or markers for children to decorate uncut sheets. Then have children glue cuttings on a sheet of construction paper to form collages.

20159425R00038

Made in the USA
Middletown, DE
09 December 2018